Copyright © 2024 by Shareem Brown

All rights reserved. No part of this publication may be reproduced, distributed, or transmitted in any form or by any means, including photocopying, recording, or other electronic or mechanical methods, without the prior written permission of the copyright owner, except in the case of brief quotations embodied in critical reviews and certain other noncommercial uses permitted by copyright law.

Illustrated by: Shalindu Malishka

Kaden and his amazing dog Suki

By
Reem Denise

Hi,
I'm Kaden James Williams.
I'm 7 years old,
and
this is my amazing dog, Suki
he's a Yorkshire Terrier.

I love to run, jump,
play tag, and catch,
but
my favorite things to do are
play football,
my favorite team is the
Buffalo Bills
and
I like to play fetch
with Suki

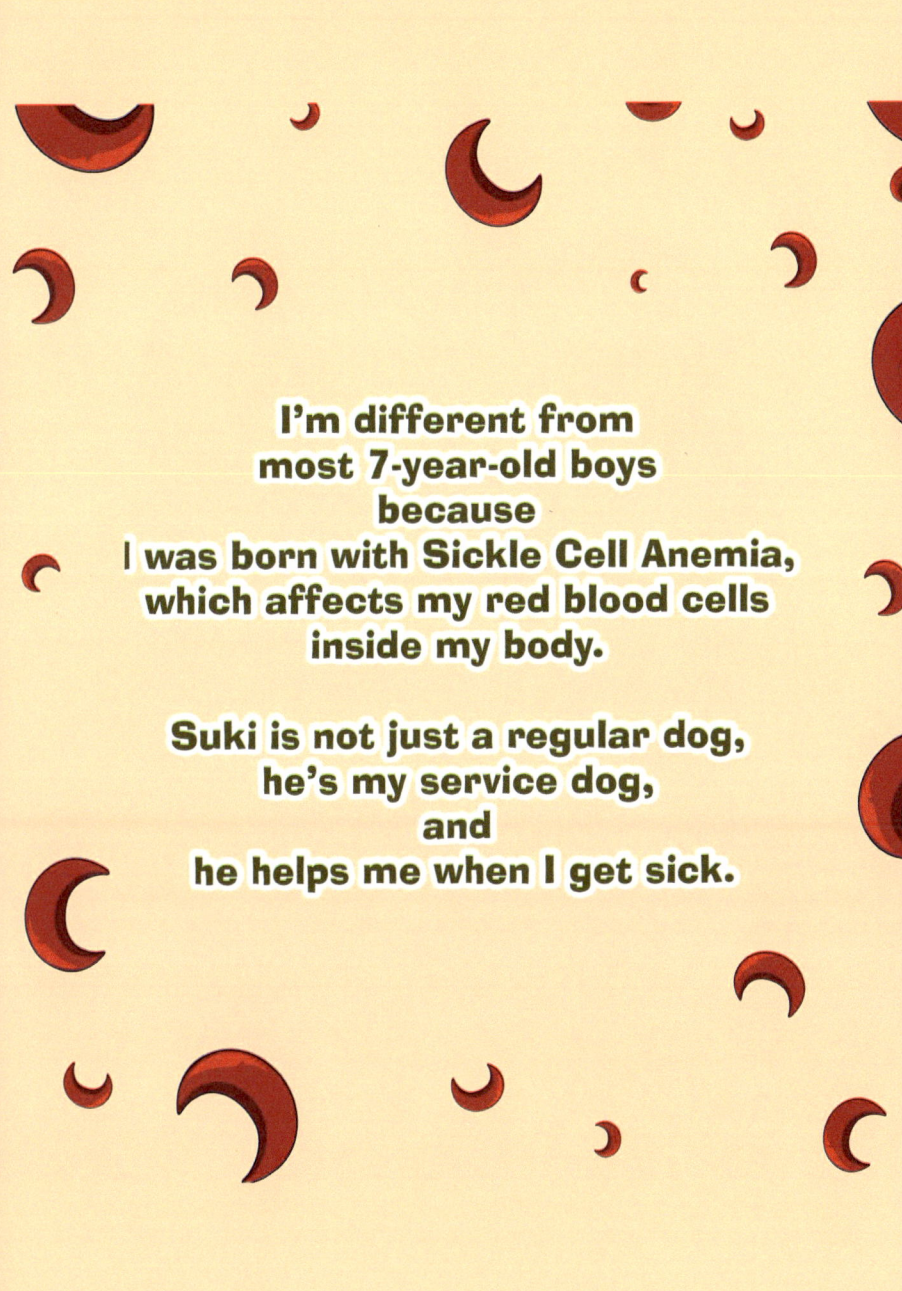

I'm different from
most 7-year-old boys
because
I was born with **Sickle Cell Anemia**,
which affects my red blood cells
inside my body.

Suki is not just a regular dog,
he's my service dog,
and
he helps me when I get sick.

I was born with
Sickle Cell Anemia
because my dad had the trait,
and so did my mom.

What is a trait, you ask?
Well, that's when both of my parents'
cells inside of their bodies are
sickle-shaped instead
of round like most people.

There is no cure for my disease yet,
but doctors and researchers are
working hard to find one.

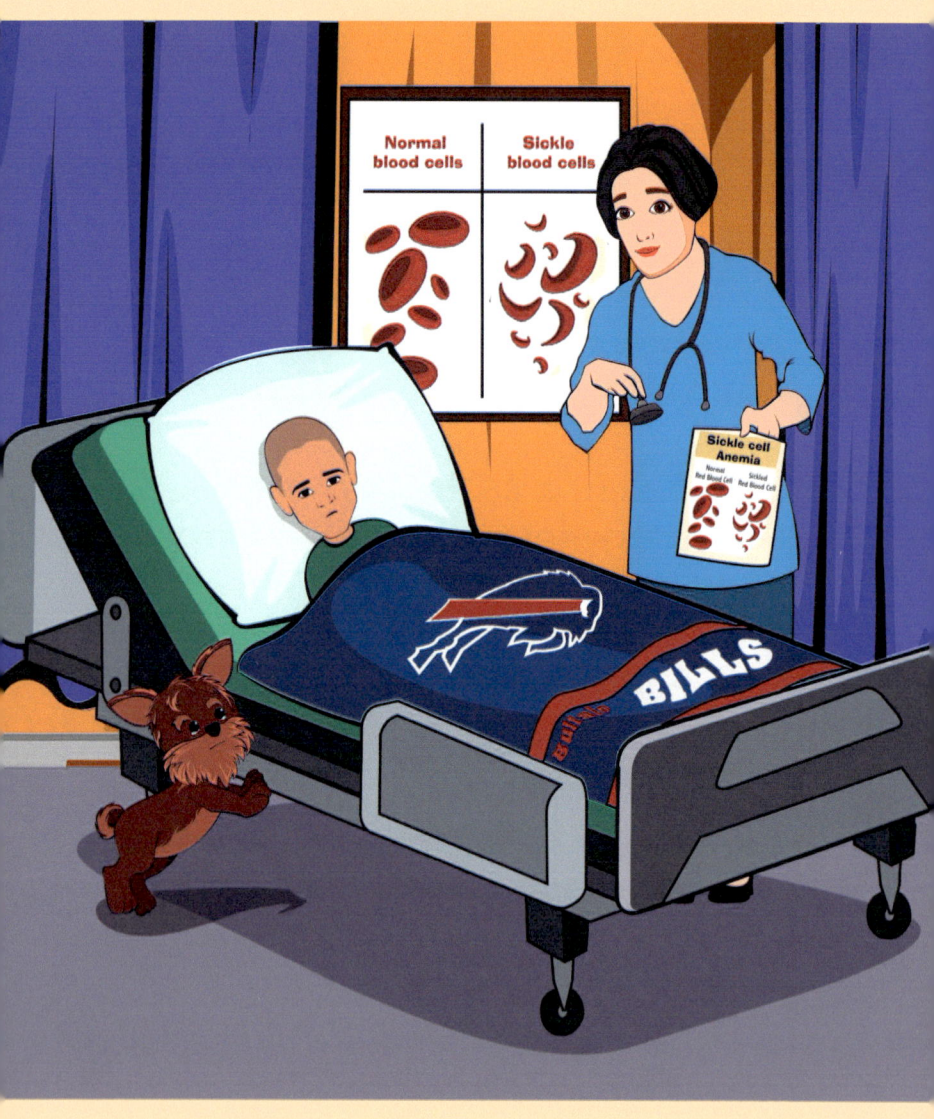

When I am in a Crisis,
I feel a lot of pain in my arms, legs,
hands, and in my feet.

I normally develop a high fever.
A Crisis is when I have a lot of pain,
and it won't stop no matter
what my mommy tries to do,
and
I usually have to go to the hospital
for a few days.

Suki can usually sense when
I am about to go into a Crisis.

He starts to breathe very heavily to let my mommy
know something is wrong with me,
or he will just sit at
my feet and not move until
Mommy comes and checks on me.

He was specially trained to do that, and
that is why he's a service dog because he does a
service for me by keeping me calm and safe.

I got Suki after my daddy died
because
he was very sick,
and then my uncle Dwayne died a few months later.
I became very sad,
and
it started to make me sick
because
I couldn't stop being sad.

Suki really helped cheer me up
and
make me happy.

When I go to the hospital,

my big sister Nisha comes to keep
me company,
and my grandma,
her name is Barbara.
We call my brother Ronnie
because
he lives in Florida.
Ronnie is also my best friend,
and
I tell him all my secrets.
He makes me laugh all the time.
When he comes to visit me,
we play video games and
dance a lot.

I have had
four blood transfusions,
which means
I had to use someone else's
blood that was donated from
the blood bank.

I've also had three surgeries.
I usually stay in the
hospital for four days
before
returning home to play with Suki,
who is always delighted
to see me.

I must take
medications every day
and night.
I can not miss any days,
or
I might get sick again.

Suki
wakes me up when it's time to
take my medicine.

One day
Mommy was walking Suki,
and
he saw a cat.
He decided he wanted to
play with the cat
and
took off running
before my mommy realized
what was going on.
He broke free from his lease
and
started chasing the cat.
My mommy tried to catch him,
but she couldn't
because
Suki was really fast.

The cat
ran across the street,
and
so did Suki,
but a car was coming,
and the driver didn't see Suki,
and
the driver accidentally
hit him with the car.
The driver stopped to check to
make sure Suki was okay,
but it was too late,
Suki had died
because
the car was way bigger
than he was.

When Mommy told me
what had happened to Suki,
we both began to cry.

I really miss my amazing dog.

My mommy
told me Suki was in Heaven
with my dad and uncle.
That makes me very happy
because
I know he is playing fetch with them,
and
they are all smiling down at me.

I want to dedicate this book to one of the strongest little boys I know, my cousin Kaden. I love you so much. I hope you know you are always a ray of sunshine in my life.

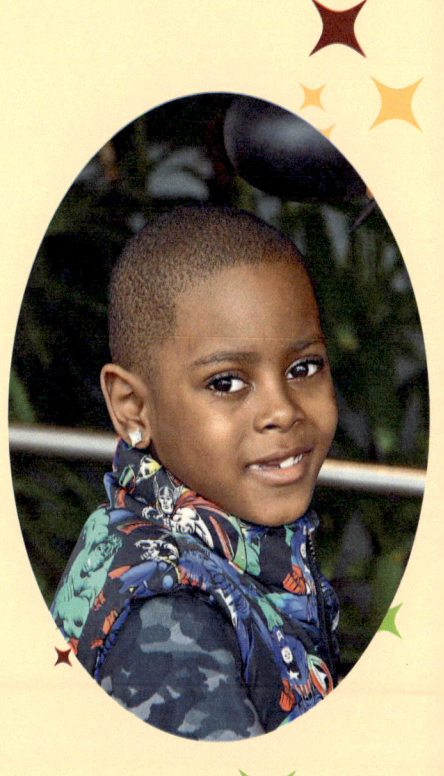

About the Author

Reem Denise, is a Mother of five and a Grandmother of fourteen, who enjoys her time making up and telling stories to her grandchildren.

Reem started telling tales of hero's and mystical lands to keep her grandchildren entertained for hours and hours, also enlisting their help to make up tales and adventures.

Reem is a substitute teacher in the Charlotte, NC area, where she enjoys working with children from Kindergarten to Fourth grade.

What would be the most fascinating part of Reem's life you ask? It is to see the joy on children's faces when she makes up stories about their lives and incorporates them in her adventures.

Made in the USA
Columbia, SC
16 June 2024